DRIVEN

The Path to Creating Your Successful Business

AUREL DAVIDYAN

TABLE OF CONTENTS

INTRODUCTION

Every one of us dreams of success. If you're like most people, you've spent quite a bit of time thinking about what success is, how you achieve it, and how good you will feel when you've achieved your goals. The part that can seem elusive is the "How you achieve success" – you know, the getting from dreaming about what you want, to having it. Everyone believes that some people get to the pinnacle of success easily. The question is, how can you be one of those people? The secret is taking the correct key steps that will help you reach your goals and accomplish what you've set out to do. In this short book, I'll walk you through each of those critical steps and explain what you need in order to achieve the success you are seeking. I will share with you some of the keys to what allowed me to become successful in my life and how they can work to help you to achieve the success that you are seeking to create in your life. So, just like in real life, lets quit talking about it and get to creating it!

CHAPTER 1

BELIEVE IN YOURSELF

Being successful is as much about self-confidence as it is about making the right moves. People who constantly doubt themselves often can't reach their goals because their negative thoughts act as saboteurs, preventing them from doing the things they want to do. That's why the first step of success is your mindset, believing in yourself. Myself, I have been told that I am arrogant when I have achieved a success and compliment myself by saying I was good at something. I always respond to such critics with the following: "Arrogance is when you <u>think</u> your good at doing something, confidence is when you <u>know</u> your good at something." In our daily society we have been taught not to compliment ourselves for a job well done. Why should we be pessimistic about our drive and abilities?

DEALING WITH PESSIMISTS AND SELF DOUBT

When you set a goal, you may find that people in your life express doubts or dismiss your goal as <u>unreasonable or unattainable</u>. You may also hear a little voice in your head that says you can't do what you want to do. Usually it is because you do not have large amounts of money or a college degree. If you want success, you've got to find a way to silence both the pessimists in your life and your negative inner critic. Listening to either can sabotage your best efforts and ensure you don't achieve success.

WITH THE PESSIMISTS, YOU'VE GOT THREE OPTIONS:

1. Ignore them and their negativity
2. Talk to them and convince them not to be negative
3. Avoid their company

The right choice may vary from person to person. Sometimes, friends and family don't realize they're being negative. When that's the case, a simple, "Hey, I'd appreciate it if you'd be positive about my goals" might do the trick.

Some people might be unwilling or unable to curb their negativity. When that's the case, you'll have to decide if you can ignore it or if you're better off avoiding their company. Choose the option that's right for you.

Avoiding the inner critic is more challenging because that critic is with you 24/7/365. A good option is to reframe the negativity and imagine that instead of talking to yourself, you're talking to a friend. You wouldn't be rude or insensitive to a friend, so don't treat yourself that way either. You are going to have good ideas and ones that will not work out as you planned or hoped for. There is only one way to never fail in life or in business, and that is to never try. We all have strengths and weaknesses; the question is what are yours.

IDENTIFYING YOUR STRENGTHS

Believing in yourself is easier when you focus on your strengths. We've all got things we do well, so why not celebrate them and embrace those things. You can cultivate a mindset of self-belief by making a list of the things you do well. Are you a great salesperson? An innovator?  A team builder? Write down your strongest traits and abilities and then turn them into affirmations. When you're heading into a meeting or negotiation or planning session, read the list and remind yourself that you're a terrific negotiator or a strong speaker. It'll put a spring in your step and help you maintain a positive outlook. Also, keep in mind that everyone else around you are also feeling nervous or are dealing with that inner critic just like you are. It is also important to be aware of your weaknesses because in doing so your weaknesses will soon become your strengths.

OVERCOMING FEARS AND NEGATIVE THOUGHTS

The flipside of acknowledging your strengths is looking at your fears, negative thoughts, or what some call weaknesses and finding ways to overcome them. We're all afraid of something. What sets us apart is how we handle those fears. There is a very powerful statement that Japanese businessmen use that I always have loved and it goes as follows; "A *intelligent man knows his strengths; a wise man knows his weaknesses.*"

With negative thoughts, try reframing them as things you would say to a friend. You can even write out your negative thoughts and then rewrite them with a positive spin.

Fears are a little trickier. You must face them. Look for ways to give yourself the tools you need to overcome your fears. For example, someone with a fear of public speaking might join a Facebook group to get critiques and encouragements from fellow members. These are some important things you can do mentally from within and then there are outside tools you can work with to help with the technical ways to increase your chances of success.

BUILDING A BUSINESS PLAN

Sometimes people fail due to a lack of planning. You'll have a better chance of achieving your goals if you lay out a concrete plan for achieving them. Writing a business plan takes time and effort. You'll need to think about your specific goals and break them down into  actionable steps. Decide what resources you'll need and how you plan to get them, and create immediate, short-term, and long-term goals.

The benefit of writing a business plan is that it will:

- Help you clarify your goals
- Make it easier to tell if you've got a goal that's too ambitious or not ambitious enough
- Help you fine-tune your ideas
- Serve as a template for approaching investors, partners, and others to talk about your business

It might be a lot of work, but the time you spend on your business plan will help you achieve success. Recently my team and I were asked by a business owner and his financial investors to give our evaluation of their business venture and create a business plan. After we took the time to evaluate the business we gave our findings to them and what they could and should do to achieve the success they were not achieving currently. One of the most important things was that they had never created a business plan before they created the business. The company had invested nearly $4 million dollars into a business and ended up with a team that had no business experience or knowledge. They had no idea how to market, where would they sell their product most effectively, not even an idea of what their profit margins should have been. Sadly, the owners were just too late in seeking the right answers to questions they did not think to ask themselves and would soon be on the road to bankruptcy.

GETTING INSPIRATION FROM SUCCESSFUL PEOPLE

When you're aiming for a goal, it's easy to get discouraged. It's easy to look at other successful people and tell yourself that you can't do what they did – or that they were more intelligent or luckier than you. The truth is that everybody struggles in some way.

You can find inspiration by seeking out stories about successful people who overcame negative thinking or other obstacles. One example is the novelist Stephen King. One of his earliest novels, *Carrie*, was rejected by more than 30 publishers before it was finally accepted. If he'd given up, he wouldn't be one of the most famous and successful authors in the world. In my own case I had created my first business at the age of 15 years old. I use this age because it was a legitimate business not some paper route or lemonade stand so many others write about when they were little children. It was an automotive service and repair shop in Portland Oregon. I reached out to many people to help raise the funds to create this but I was too young and I was an immigrant and thus no bank loans were available to me and I was rejected many times. I simply did not give up and found ways to fund my business and within the following two years I had built the business up so well I was approached to sell it and I did sell the business for a very large profit.

Did you know that Bill Gates had a failed company before he started Microsoft and that

Walt Disney was fired by the Kansas City Star because his editor said he lacked imagination and had no good ideas? The point here is if you let others hold you back, you won't be successful. The only way to succeed is to **believe in yourself first and foremost.**

CHAPTER 2

TEST IDEAS TO PROVE THEY ARE GOOD

You probably have tons of ideas. Some are good and some are not good. How can you tell the difference? Simple, test your ideas!

WHY IS TESTING IDEAS AND/OR PRODUCTS SO IMPORTANT?

Testing your ideas and/or products is essential – it's not that hard to understand why. Which would you rather do:

1. Spend your time, and money, developing and launching a product only to find out that it doesn't sell the way you thought it would; or
2. Spend some time testing and refining your idea before you invest your hard-earned dollars in launching it.

The answer's a resounding test it. It's a better use of your time and money to test things out first. Once you've tested, refined your idea, and re-tested it, you'll have a pretty good idea of whether it's going to work or not. Keep in mind that business is not emotional. I have seen many business owners become emotional and fall in love with a business idea and not test it against factual research and lose thousands or even millions of dollars.

MARKET RESEARCH

One way to improve your chances of success is to do *market research* before you spend valuable time and money trying to start your business. That might mean pitching your idea to a few friends or family members. It might mean asking your blog readers what they think of it or on your social media pages or in groups or even researching using Google Trends©.

With products, it's a little trickier. But you might do a Google© search for products in your niche or spend a few minutes on Amazon© seeing what's available. If there's a product that does exactly what yours will do, you'll need to tweak it a little.

The most important thing with testing ideas is to make sure you've got a unique value proposition. **That's the one thing your product or idea has that nobody else has!**

Your value proposition could be about functionality or it could be about price. The main thing is to know how you'll differentiate your product from others on the market. One of the ways to come up with your products value proposition is to do a **SWOT analysis**. This is a marketing tool that stands for <u>Strengths, Weaknesses, Opportunities, Threats.</u> This practice will help you to identify problems and thus see if you can create a solution or if there is no solution thus no idea for a business which will save you a great deal of money and heart ache.

IDENTIFYING PROBLEMS AND FINDING SOLUTIONS

You're more likely to succeed if you identify a product, or service, that provides a solution to a problem faced by your target audience. People are always going online to find answers and researching purchases that they are considering. They ask questions and look for products that will help them. You can find problems by searching a common keyword in your niche and looking at Google's suggested searches. For example, say you want to create a project in the pet training niche and you're looking for an angle for puppy training product. You might search "How to house train a puppy" and see this:

You can see there are some ideas there, including focusing on training with a bell or training with a crate. You might be able to carve out a niche for yourself by focusing on a training method for people who work during the day. That's a problem that might not be addressed by other products – and that means it could be your unique value proposition!

SETTING GOALS/SMALL STEPS TO SUCCESS

Do you know how to set goals? Setting a goal involves more than just saying "I want a successful business." You may have heard about *SMART goals*. It means setting goals that are **Specific, Measurable, Attainable, Reasonable, and Timely**.

This book is about achieving a successful mindset, but "success" isn't a specific enough word when you're setting goals. Here are some examples of SMART goals:

- Incorporate a new business
- Generate $500,000 in revenue in the first year
- Attract 100 new customers in the first quarter

What you'll notice is that these goals are all specific and achievable – and in the case of the revenue and client-based goals, they're measurable and timely, too. When you set goals, ask if they're SMART and if they're not, fine-tune them until they are.

PLANNING FOR FAILURE

You're probably thinking it is insane to plan for failure. But, planning for failure is also a smart thing to do. Everybody fails. I have never met a single successful entrepreneur in my entire career that has not had a failure on the way to being successful. Remember the story about Stephen King being rejected 30+ times by publishers? The reason he's the highly successful author we know today is because what he did after those rejections.

He didn't stop. He didn't give up. He learned to cope with rejection, and he persisted. Before you start, ask yourself what you'll do if you fail. Keep asking and plan for it. Understand that you will fail at some of the steps that you take on your journey to success – and know that you're still in the game unless you take yourself out of it.

Next, we'll talk about one of the most important steps and states of mind to achieve your success, which is related to failure. Successful people learn from their mistakes. You will learn how you can, too. Just as I had mentioned earlier in this book, there is only one way to never fail and that is if you never try. True, you will never fail, but you will never even get the chance to succeed.

CHAPTER 3

LEARNING FROM MISTAKES

Every cloud has a silver lining and so does every mistake. It's a bit cliché to say that mistakes are learning opportunities, but the fact is that it is a simple reality. Just like failure, mistakes show us who we are. We all make mistakes. It's what you do after you make a mistake that makes the difference between success and failure.

I had a friend that created an innovative technology in 2001 and it was ahead of its time and he got the opportunity to pitch his idea to venture capitalists in San Francisco. These were one of the most well know VC firms in the world at the time. During his meeting and his pitch 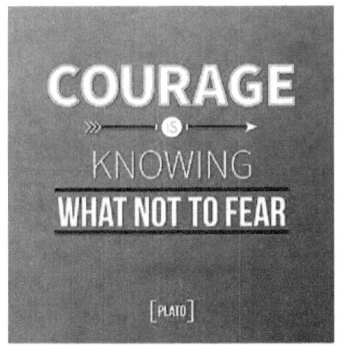 one of the principles on the board, a man worth billions of dollars, asked him if he had ever had a business failure in his career. My friend took a nervous swallow and responded that he had failed in one of his first businesses. My friend was sure that this would be the end of the meeting for them but felt he had to be honest in his answer.

Needless to say, they got an offer to fund them of $13 million dollars. My friend asked the man later why he asked him if he had ever had a failed business and the man responded to him that he only considered investing in businesses with managers that had failed in the past because it was the best teacher in business.

WHY START-UPS FAIL

It's not easy to get a start-up off the ground. When start-ups fail, it can be for any one of several reasons. Here are some of the most common:

- Not focusing on customers and solving their problems
- Lack of focus
- Scaling too quickly
- Not building a success team

We've already talked about focusing on customers. If you do that, you'll be halfway to success because you won't be thinking about yourself, you'll be thinking about your audience.

Focus problems happen when you try to do too many things at once. The saying of **"Jack of all trades, master of none"** is very true. Simplifying goals and focusing on one product or idea will help keep your eyes on the prize. Scaling is something that can send any entrepreneur into a tailspin. Allow your business to grow organically and scale only when you're ready. Business growth is wonderful but if not managed correctly it will tear a business to pieces. We'll talk about how to build a success team later – but suffice to say, you can't do everything yourself or by being afraid of making mistakes!

REFRAMING MISTAKES AS OPPORTUNITIES

Nobody likes making mistakes. It stinks to be wrong. But, every successful entrepreneur needs to get comfortable with it – and learn to see mistakes as opportunities. What happens when you mess up? If you pay attention, you can learn something, everything you learn now will help you with your next goal.

When you make a mistake, take a deep breath and ask:

"What can I learn from this?"

Then, once you've identified it, use the lesson to create your next opportunity. Once you get in the habit of doing it, it'll be easy every time following.

TIGHTENING GOALS

We already talked about SMART goals. When you don't achieve a goal, it's easy to feel discouraged and even beaten. Often, it's just a sign that your goal was too big. If you've ever made a to-do list, you may have noticed how gratifying it is to cross out the items on it. Some people even put simple things on their lists because they know they'll be able to complete them quickly.

When you set goals for yourself, take every long-term goal and break it down into the smallest possible steps. Just like when you go on a road trip across the country, you do not look at the map of your destination like New York City, you look at the first 100 miles of the trip where you will need to get fuel. It is easier to do things in smaller digestible chunks. Focus on what you want and narrow your goals to help you achieve it. You'll be far more likely to get where you want to go if you have tight, achievable goals.

HOW TO FIND THE LESSONS IN YOUR EXPERIENCES

Everything you experience is a lesson. When you make a mistake, or fail, it's natural to be upset. Take time to be upset. But then, step back. Ask what you did wrong, and what you would do differently next time. If you lack information, go find it. Read, research, study, talk to other people in your industry – and then take what you've learned to heart and use it in the future.

SPLIT TESTING

One of the best ways to refine your goals and fine-tune your product or service is with *split testing*. Split testing involves taking content, or an ad campaign, and testing different versions until you get the best results. The key to split testing is testing only one element at a time. Not satisfied with your Facebook© ad? Test two different headlines, choose the one that performs better, and then split test your call to action.

CREATING YOUR PLAN B

It's always a good idea to have a Plan B. If your first idea doesn't work, what will you try next? There's no shame in having a back-up plan. In fact, part of the reason that successful people become successful is that they have back-up plans! I have always touted the saying Options, Options, Options.

Next, we'll talk about how to keep focused on your customers, so you don't get off track.

CHAPTER 4

FOCUS ON YOUR CUSTOMERS

"The customer is always right." That's a truism of customer service, but in today's digital economy the saying is more linked to "the customer is always willing to have a conversation to come to a thoughtful and mutually satisfying outcome."

In the previous chapter, you learned that one of the main reasons start-ups fail is because they fail to focus on the customer. But you're not going to make that mistake, correct?

WHY YOU SHOULD FOCUS ON WHAT CUSTOMERS WANT/NEED

Customers are the life blood of your business. If they're not happy, your business will fail. It's that simple. In today's social media channel-based world, there is no reason that your customer should be unhappy or ignored. Your mindset for success means that you have

the chance to share and communicate directly with your customers, do not let that chance slip you by.

We've already talked about market research and testing. Even after you've tested everything, though, you still need to focus on your customers. It doesn't matter what critics of your company and products say. If your customers are happy and satisfied, you'll grow and you will make money. Think about the famous sign during Bill Clinton's presidential campaign. It read, "It's the economy, stupid." It was a reminder that the campaign's voters – its customers – were worried about the economy. Keeping their focus on the community helped make the campaign win.

CREATING A GREAT START-TO-FINISH EXPERIENCE

A customer's experience with you starts when they first learn about your company, or product, and continues for as long as they use your product. When you think about the customer experience, think through every step of the experience. This is called the sales funnel in marketing departments. It starts from the type of advertising that you create to how and where your customer interacts you're your product or service and all the way too how they are treated long after the sale is completed. Offer stellar content, an easy buying process, and excellent support. Customers who've received top-notch support remember it. They'll mention it to their friends. In the same, if your customers receive bad service or support they will share that with friends and in today's digital and social world potential customers around the globe instantly and bad news or reviews is statistically shared ten times more than good reviews. So, be aware.

PROVIDING VALUE

I am regularly asked "what's the secret to attracting customers?" My answer is always the same; **VALUE**. Before anybody spends their money on your product, they're going to want to know that it'll deliver on its promises. You can make them feel better about that by offering clear value to them even before they buy. That means creating and delivering interesting, informative, relevant, and actionable content that'll help you engage their attention.

Delivering value, triggers a mental glitch called *Reciprocity*. When you give a customer something for **FREE** – even if it's information – they're more likely to feel comfortable buying from you. If the information you give free to your potential customers, and everyone is your potential customer, you are no longer perceived as just a business looking to get their money but as a considerate entity almost like a friend if the information is helpful to them.

Of course, value must come from your product as well. It includes the quality of the product, its usefulness, its longevity, and its price.

BECOMING AN AUTHORITY/EXPERT

People look up to authority figures or experts about something. You can prove your authority/expertise by doing what we just talked about – delivering value to your customers.

But authority is more than that. It's about showing that you're a reliable and knowledgeable source of information. In social media, it means delivering original content that's informative and actionable. It may also mean curating content from industry publications and authorities and sharing it with your own synopsis on the topic. One way to establish yourself as an authority is to offer a lead magnet to grow your list. A lead magnet can be a short eBook, a tip sheet, a template, or anything else that demonstrates your expertise. You still will have to support your expertise long after the sale.

CUSTOMER SUPPORT

Customer support starts when a customer first visits your website or finds your business during the researching phase. You should think about what kind of support your customers need and how you'll deliver it. In the days before the internet, support was mostly in person or on the phone. Today, you may want to think about:

- Email support
- Chat support
- Chatbots
- Self-service options
- FAQ
- Social media support

You'll need to test various options to figure out what'll work for your audience. Remember that most companies are merging social media with support and you should consider you will need to build one as well. With all the tools and channels and states of mind you can cultivate for a successful business, you still will need to build a great team.

CHAPTER 5

BUILDING YOUR SUCCESS TEAM

If you want to be successful, you won't get there alone. There's a temptation to do that, of course. Wearing every possible hat might save you a little money. But in the end, it'll cost you more in time (and sanity) than the alternative.

WHY YOU SHOULDN'T TRY TO DO EVERYTHING

You might have a lot of skills. Perhaps you're a great innovator with excellent communication skills. Maybe you've dabbled in accounting and flirted with marketing. No matter how good you are, you're not equally good at everything. I refer to the saying of "Jack of all trades, master none". If you try to do the things you're not so great at, you might wind up settling for a less-than-perfect result or failure. Many entrepreneurs do everything at first. You might need to. But once you've established your business and product, it's a good idea to branch out and get some help. Not only will you be able to do a better job at the things that ONLY you can do, you'll also be able to live a balanced and productive life – and that's part of success.

TIPS FOR BUILDING A TEAM

The idea of building a team can be an intimidating one, particularly if you're thinking that you need to hire people and deal with taxes and insurance. The good news is that you don't need to do those things unless you want to. Lots of companies outsource tasks as needed without hiring full-time or even part-time people. The first step is deciding who you need on your team. Are you struggling to keep up with social media? You may want to outsource it to someone with more experience. Perhaps you need a bookkeeper to come in once a week to pay bills. Maybe you need a payroll service. You may decide to hire someone full time. Keep in mind, though, that there are plenty of tasks you can outsource to freelancers. There are many sites that makes it easy to find virtual assistants and team members.

THE IMPORTANCE OF DELEGATION

How do you know what to do yourself and what to delegate? Delegation is an essential skill. You know you can't do everything, but it can be difficult to let go of the things you're accustomed to doing even when you have help.

Here are some questions to help you learn how to delegate. About each task, ask:

- Can I teach someone else to do it?

- Is there anything that I'm unable to teach?
- Is my personal input required?
- Do I have someone on my team who's capable of learning how to do it?

Unless the task absolutely requires your input and skills, it should be open to delegation. Yes, you'll need to spend some time training your staff, or freelancers, to do the task to your standards. You'll probably end up fielding a few questions and possibly, correcting a few mistakes. There's nothing wrong with you keeping key tasks to yourself, but your goal should be to maximize efficiency while also prioritizing accuracy. It can also be helpful to take an inventory of your team's skills. They might have abilities you don't know about yet. There are a million great business ideas but I have not met one banker or VC board that has not stated that they do not invest in businesses, they invest in management teams – the people running the business. You will be highly successful in your business if you work through knowing your product or service, not being afraid to take calculated risks, stop listening to the critics especially you, developing a business team and delegating. With all of that said there is one additional thing here that you need to investigate and try to master at best, that is leadership skills. Keep in mind that your customers are always watching and listening to you and your companies dialogue. More importantly, your team is listening to your words and actions better known as your Leadership. So, it is a good idea to learn it and strengthen it now.

LEADERSHIP SKILLS

Everyone has had the experience of working for a nasty or mean boss. While it's common for people to be promoted, or become a business owner, into management when they excel, in non-leadership positions, the truth is that a lot of the people who are in positions of power or leadership don't have  the skills they need to effectively manage a team. In other words, they lack the "must-have" leadership skills that all great bosses or entrepreneurs have in common. The good news is that they're skills you can easily learn. I'll explain the top essential leadership skills you need to successfully manage a team, and how to set yourself up for long-term success whether you're working for yourself or for corporate America. The top essential leadership skills are:

Communication, Adaptability, Team Building, Strategic Thinking, and Delegation.

COMMUNICATION

Without proper, clear, and concise communication, you can't hope to become an effective leader or even be a person that others will ever listen to. Communication is your best tool for explaining your ideas, setting expectations, and building your team. I will explain why strong communication skills are essential for leaders and share some tips about how to communicate effectively both in writing and in person.

You might be sitting there reading this and the first thought you may think to yourself is "Why are communications so important to know?" Let me put it this way, if communicating or learning how to do it well is not important then why does every single college and university in the world require students to take a communications class to obtain their degrees. Outside of the college world it is said that 90% of all highly successful individuals read voraciously and learn, from reading, the art of communicating with people.

"THE IMPORTANCE OF INTERPERSONAL COMMUNICATION"

Interpersonal communication is what builds relationships. If you listen to employees complain about their bosses and employers, one of the top issues they're dealing with is usually lack of a direct and clear channel of communication. Of course, communication goes both ways. But, as a leader, it's your job to set the tone for interaction within your organization or team.

Effective communication:

- Minimizes misunderstandings and confusion
- Ensures that team members know what you expect
- Encourages communication among team members
- Increases the chances that you'll reach your goals

Any time you touch base with your team, or with a client, you're using communication skills. That means every phone call, every meeting, every chat, and every email reflects your ability to communicate and keep a pulse on how projects are going.

TIPS FOR EFFECTIVE COMMUNICATION IN WRITING AND OFF THE CUFF

What makes for effective communication? The hallmarks of a good communication are clarity, detail, sincerity, and honesty.

<u>Clarity</u>: Means that you must be able to articulate what you want in a way that the person you're talking to can understand. You're not communicating effectively if the listener or reader can't understand what you need or expect from them.

<u>Detail</u>: Means that you are specific about what you want, expect, or need to know. If you delegate a task and the team member still has questions about what to do or how to do the job, your communication skills have fallen short.

<u>Sincerity</u>: Means that If you do not communicate from the heart and invoke your passion into what you are sharing with others, whatever your message is will fall on deaf ears.

<u>Honesty</u>: Means that you must be truthful when communicating with your team. That doesn't mean you need to tell them everything you're thinking all the time, but it does mean that you cannot mislead them or deliberately omit information that might help them achieve the goals you've laid out for the team.

Here are a few tips for communicating effectively:

- In writing, keep your sentences and paragraphs short
- Think about what you say before you say it

- Always keep your audience in mind. Don't use jargon unless you're sure they'll understand it
- Pay attention to how the listener reacts to what you say
- Be available to answer questions and patient while you do it

These tips will help you be an effective communicator and enhance your ability to lead. Next, I will talk about why you must be adaptable to any, and every situation, in order to become a great leader.

ADAPTABILITY

You've heard the term "survival of the fittest". It's the principle that tells us that only those who can handle change and cope with adversity survive. In other words, adaptability is necessary – and it can mean the difference between success and failure in your business and in your life. Let's discuss why great leaders must be adaptable, and provide some tips about how you can increase your adaptability and learn to go with the flow.

HOW ADAPTABILITY CAN HELP YOU SUCCEED

In our professional lives, things seldom go the way we want them to. There are too many variables for that to always be the case and often, the things that derail our career, or our personal lives, feels as though it's out of our control.

There have been many times in my life when I've had an expectation that hasn't been met – and I'm willing to bet that's true for you, too.

In one of my most successful businesses that I have ever created, and am still managing and growing daily, placed me in a situation where my expectations were shattered. I had brought in a very knowledgeable business partner and I expected that this move would allow the company to grow beyond my experience and knowledge. In the end I was put into a position where I had to adapt and buy the partner out for many times more than it was worth. I adapted to the situation and learned a lesson and have grown the company a thousand percent more than what I had to pay to get my company back. The bottom line is that what you do in the face of adversity is what'll determine whether you're able to quickly recover then reset and get back on the path to success.

If you have a setback, do you get up and keep going – or do you give up and move onto something else? Great leaders learn to go with the flow. They understand that success doesn't happen overnight. Their adaptability helps them get through failure and come out the other side a winner.

TIPS FOR INCREASING ADAPTABILITY AND GOING WITH THE FLOW

Some people have a high level of adaptability, naturally. If that's you, then you're probably in good shape. But what if it's not? What if you're easily discouraged or daunted by setbacks? Is there anything you can do to increase your adaptability?

YES!

Here are some tips to help you increase your adaptability and go with the flow.

1. Make contingency plans. You should always have a Plan B. It doesn't mean you're planning for failure. Instead, it means that you've given thought to what you'll do if Plan A doesn't go as planned.

2. Practice resilience. If you're like most people, you probably experience tons of small setbacks. When one happens, pay attention to how you react and think about how you can switch up your internal monologue to be more positive.

3. Come up with a daily affirmation to remind yourself that you can deal with disappointment. You might try something like, "Even if things don't go my way today, I'm going to keep going and not get bogged down by it."

4. When something goes wrong, don't react immediately. Take a few deep breaths and let yourself feel the disappointment. A lot of times, we get wrapped up in disappointment because we're trying too hard to overcome it. It's okay to feel disappointed – but it's not okay to let it get the best of you.

These tips can help you learn to be more resilient. Even a big disappointment or a disappointing failure doesn't have to mean that your goals are out of reach.

Now that we have discussed adaptability let's talk about how to build a team – something that's very important for every leader.

TEAM BUILDING

We'll always reach a higher level of success with a team. Even the self-made millionaires and billionaires out there didn't do it entirely on their own. Bill Gates is a great example. Yes, he had a great idea when he created Windows – but he had a talented team of programmers, designers, writers, marketers, and administrators to help him launch it. Team-building is an essential leadership skill, and how you can recognize the areas where you need help so you can build a powerhouse team of your own is one of the most valuable skills to have.

THE BENEFITS OF BUILDING A STRONG TEAM

As hard as you may work and as determined as you may be, you can't do everything on your own, nor should you. It's not practical, and it's not working smarter – it's working harder. Consider the phrase, "Jack of all trades, master of none." You might be great at some things, but chances are there are areas in your business that would benefit from outside support.

You might be tempted to try to do everything yourself, telling yourself that you'll save money. A lot of entrepreneurs make that mistake and it leads to failure. They undervalue their time and energy and underestimate how hard it will be to wear every hat, every day. Choosing a team means that you'll have ongoing support within your own customized network. You can delegate tasks – something we'll talk about later – and have time to do the things you do best. You'll also be able to enjoy other aspects of life because, let's face it, you'll work better if you make time to play, too. The trick, of course, is building the right team.

TIPS FOR ATTRACTING TEAM MEMBERS AND KNOWING WHEN YOU NEED HELP

You need a team, but where you do you start? The first step is identifying the key areas where you need help. If you're building a business, you'll need to build a brand, create products, design your website, structure mailing lists, attract new clients, service those clients, and so on.

Start by looking at the things you do very well. Maybe you're a killer salesperson or a master communicator. Those may be things you can do on your own.

Next, look at the things that aren't in your wheelhouse. Maybe you have very little marketing experience or you're not great at organization. The first team members you hire should be the people who can help you with your weaknesses. You'll have the best chance of success if you use this method. The next thing you need to do is attract the right team members.

To do that, you'll need to:

- Write accurate and attractive job descriptions.
- Offer fair payment.

- Place ads to help team members find you or look for them on sites like LinkedIn.
- Interview people.

Make sure that you ask for samples of their work where it's appropriate and check their references. These days, it's easy to hire people to work remotely without ever meeting them. You should set up Skype interviews with anyone you don't plan to meet in person. It's also a good idea to impose a probation period on any new hires. That way, you'll be able to make changes easily if you need to. Just make sure to put everything in writing. Now, we need to talk about strategic thinking.

STRATEGIC THINKING

Strategy thinking is an essential element of leadership. I'll explain why and give you some tips for improving your strategic thinking and planning skills. The Role of Strategy in Success

Strategy is simply long-term planning with a fancy name. You have a goal in mind and then you map out a step-by-step plan to achieve it. If you want it to work, your strategy must be logical and practical. Each step you take should build to the next step.

Without strategy, it's very difficult – maybe even impossible – to achieve your biggest goals. You might have the goal to be the CEO of a Fortune 500 company. Your strategy might include getting an MBA and a host of other steps that will put you in a position to achieve that goal.

The thing about strategy is that it's not just for you. Having a strategy in place can help you get investors to fund your company, and it can also help you inspire your team.

TIPS FOR IMPROVING YOUR STRATEGIC THINKING AND PLANNING AHEAD

Some people have a natural gift for strategic thinking. They're the people who are great chess players and who naturally seem to see everything 10 steps ahead. If you're not one of them, don't worry. Here are some tips to help you improve your strategic thinking.

- Before you make any decision, think about some possible outcomes and brainstorm what you'll do next with each one. This is the kind of practical thinking that can help you become a better strategist.
- Think about your goals and work backwards to figure out what actions will help you achieve them. Think of this as reverse-engineering a strategy.
- Ask team members and trusted friends for suggestions to help you plan strategically.
- Try creating a timeline to plan each step on the way to your goal.

The more you practice strategic thinking, the easier it will be.

Now we'll talk about the last, but not least, must-have leadership skill: delegation.

DELEGATION

In some ways, delegation is the most important skill of them all. I've already touched on some reasons why it's important not to try to do everything yourself. The key to making that happen is to learn how to delegate effectively. I will explain why delegation is important and provide some tips to help you delegate the right tasks to the right people.

WHY YOU SHOULDN'T TRY TO DO EVERYTHING YOURSELF

If you want to be a great leader, you need to know how to delegate tasks and – just as importantly – *who* to delegate them to. You might have a ton of energy and the will to do everything yourself, but as I said before, it's not always an effective strategy. Not only will you be shouldering the responsibility for tasks that aren't in your wheelhouse, but you also run the risk of burning out. We all need down time – and we all do our best work when we're focused on what we're good at and love to do. Delegation allows you to focus your time and energy on the things you're best it and the things that only you can do. That means you'll have more time to lead because you won't be burned out from trying to do everything.

TIPS TO HELP YOU DECIDE WHAT TO DELEGATE TO OTHERS

The trick to great delegation is knowing two things:

1. Which tasks and jobs can be delegated; and
2. Who should handle those tasks.

So, let's take each of these things in turn, starting with knowing which tasks to delegate. You should delegate:

- Things that your team members excel at
- Things they can be taught to do
- Things that don't require your personal input

It might be useful to start by identifying the things that only you can do. These may include making strategic decisions about your team or meeting with investors. Then, make a list of the things you can delegate. Once you've got the list, it's time to think about who the best people are for those jobs. Here are some questions to ask:

- Which team members already have skills that make them suitable for the task?
- Which team members have shown aptitude for core skills, like communication, teamwork, or logic?
- Which team members are eager to learn and willing to take on something new?

Any of these questions can help you identify people who are ready to handle the tasks and responsibilities you've identified. Once you've identified the people you need, you should spend some time thinking about the training and support they'll need to succeed with their delegated tasks. You may need to spend some one-on-one time with them or pay someone else to train them. They may need an outside class or seminar.

Delegate the tasks, and make sure that you communicate clearly and in detail about what you expect from each team member. Make yourself available to answer questions, and most importantly, keep in mind that they may not get it right on the first try.

There's a chance that you may need to adapt along the way. You might not pick the best team member for every task on your first try. The key is to keep an open mind, listen, and be patient. You'll need all your leadership skills to decide what to delegate, choose the best people for each job, and guide them along the way to success. That's why I saved delegation for last – because it's a skill that necessarily incorporates all the others we've discussed.

AFTERWORD

When I began my entrepreneurial career nearly twelve years ago, I did not have anyone in the background telling me what moves to make or even encouragement. I come from a very loving but stern and cautious family. Our culture is not one that advises or even encourages taking big risks in one's professional life. I am not judging or referring to my family in a negative way at all. The one thing my family did teach me was to have a good work ethic and to have faith in my beliefs. I have been blessed to have some of the greatest teachers and friends that I could have ever hoped for that have shared great insights that they have learned over the years and have saved me a great deal of pain by not having to learn those lessons by making costly mistakes. I have learned many great lessons via my mistakes and through my successes alike. When I decided to write this book, it was in the hopes that my story and experiences might be able to create time saving lessons for anyone looking to take the chance to achieve their success in business and life.

I believe that if you have faith in yourself and a higher power and are willing to listen to those around you that have learned from experience then you will have the chance to create your very own successful life in business. Yes, it is true that it takes more than just the items I have shared here in these pages. It takes these factors and tools that all can be learned but it also takes passion, intelligence, and love. Yes, I said love.

If you do not know how to love yourself and others then you really will not ever feel passion for anything in life beyond money. I can tell you first hand that if your only love is for money and you make money your god, you will soon enough be separated from your love and come away empty and lost. Money is great and it can make the journey of life more enjoyable but it is simply just paper and metal. Money has only the power that we give it, both good and bad.

I am inspired by the many wonderful friends and colleagues I have had help me to be inspired and write this book. I am thankful for my family and children that inspire me daily to be an example they are proud of. I wish you all the best results and thank you for believing in me enough to read this book.

Aurel Davidyan